WHAT IS A DATABASE?

FUNDAMENTALS OF A RELATIONAL DATABASE

GREG L. TURNQUIST

MOUNTAIN
SUMMIT PRESS

CONTENTS_

Greg L. Turnquist

c/o What Is A Database?

P.O. Box 4042

Clarksville, TN 37043

USA

ISBN: 978-1-956410-43-3 (e-book)

ISBN: 978-1-956410-44-0 (paperback)

ISBN: 978-1-956410-45-7 (hardback)

This book is dedicated to those that strive to continue learning, day after day, even if they may be experts in their fields. For the day we stop learning is the day we falter.

PREFACE_

> "If you know what's going on, you'll know what to do."
>
> - NELSON NASH

This book was originally conjured up literally in a dream. Hard at work writing content for our CockroachDB customers, I had fallen sleep that night, after work, and dreamed I was in some lecture hall. And I happened to be talking about the fundamentals of relational databases.

With our customers, we are always striving to find the right balance between discussing first principle concepts of relational databases vs. explaining how they manifest in our specific database engine. In the dream, it felt as if someone had asked, "Why does SQL act like that?" And I was deep diving into why it really can't be any other way!

I woke up, feeling strangely satisfied at having given such a presentation, only to realize it hadn't happened at all!

But that didn't mean it *couldn't* happen.

Later that day, I shared this idea with my manager, and he seemed excited. So in my spare time I just started writing.

I first saw this as a live stream to host on YouTube. Something that was perhaps 3-4 hours long, where I would explain, bit-by-bit, what naturally arises when you put data together relationally. I hadn't realized it, but the more I discuss relational databases, the more I could see not just *how* to use them...but in fact *why* they work the way they do.

In truth, relational databases and SQL are, as a former colleague of mine once said, "not rocket science." And the more you use tables and queries, the more apparent it becomes how these concepts fit together.

This nature of SQL and relational databases is quite possibly a scientific fact, that is a *computer* scientific fact. The nature of one-to-many relationships and their aspects we see every day in SQL may be a **reality** when it comes to data.

There is the big reason that despite being over fifty years old, relational databases are still the prevailing data storage paradigm of choice in this day and age.

WHAT IS A DATABASE?_

20 years of NoSQL advocacy, and developers still reach for relational databases 80% of the time. This book will dive into what makes relational databases tick. It explores the core features of a relational database. And hopefully, you'll have a better grounding in why SQL works the way it does!

For starters, it's important to clarify the difference between a "database" (DB) vs. a "relational database management system" (RDBMS).

If we were to build a system that involved serving up **books** in a library, then the **database** would be all the information about the books and how to loan them out. The engine that houses that database is a separate thing and something we'll only mention when needed.

Every database has a name. It doesn't matter what the name is. This is simply to give us a handle on referencing the database, and to distinguish it from other databases that the database engine may be servicing.

In our case, we could name it LIBRARY.

To store data in a database, we must begin with the database's most basic element: **tables**.

WHAT IS A TABLE?_

Tables, simply put, are reams of information stored in tabular format. Visualize a spreadsheet. While the entire file could be deemed your database, each worksheet with its own tabular collection of information would denote a **table**.

Again, if you imagine a library filled with millions of books, you can imagine a **table** named BOOK that contains one row for every **book** that is available to purchase.

- Dune => Frank Herbert
- Spring Data => Mark Pollack etc.

This bullet list represents, in the simplest way possible, two distinct entries of data.

We could have other tables. For example, we could capture other aspects of our library including publishers, due dates, and types of books (hardcover, paperback). What sort of tables of information would you add to manage a library?

One aspect of a table is that it has a consistent nature to it. The BOOK table represents book-related data. An AUTHOR table could be used to capture author-related information.

Once this is agreed upon, then it's implicit that author-based data isn't stored in the BOOK table, and book-based data isn't stored in the AUTHOR table. After all, if you have that spreadsheet we just mentioned at the beginning of this chapter, would you put an **author** entry into the **book** worksheet?

The "thing" each table represents is known as its **entity** type. People will sketch out **entities** on a whiteboard and show how these entities relate to each other. Then they will *implement* those entities with **table definitions**.

Do we know enough about what a database is to do that?

Not quite. First, we need to understand **rows**.

WHAT IS A ROW?_

The BOOK table we just alluded to, if it represented our stock of books, would have one row of data for every book available for checkout.

It's easy to imagine a table containing a row for *Dune* by Frank Herbert, a row for *Spring Data* by Mark Pollack, and a row for any other book available for checkout in our library.

It's important to understand that every entry in the BOOK table is a separate row.

Now in describing the rows of a table, we hinted at some attributes. Let's go back to *Dune* by Frank Herbert. In describing that book, we have described both the **title** and its **author**. What other attributes does a book have?

- Year it was published
- Company that published it
- Status (AVAILABLE, CHECKED OUT, BACK ORDERED, ...)
- Number of copies
- Number of times it's been checked out

In fact, we can imagine many attributes. In a relational database, each of these attributes is called a **column**.

WHAT IS A COLUMN?_

When you print out a table in a tabular format, and you see a separate row for each entry, the attributes occupy **columns**. They're just like the fields you find in a data type in your application.

It's important to understand that in relational databases, each column of a table can only contain one value.

"What if I need more than one value?"

Great question!

The short answer is that you actually need another table related to this one. We'll get to that in a moment, but the other characteristic you need to know is that every **table** in a relational database has a **table definition** that spells out the data type for every **column**. And when you gather *all* the table definitions, they are known as that database's **schema**.

We just mentioned that sometimes a given row of data needs *multiple* values in one of its columns. For example, imagine a book that has more than one author. *Spring Data* published in 2012 has several authors including Mark Pollack, Thomas Risberg, Oliver Drotbohm, Jonathon Brisbin, and Michael Hunger.

Because we can't assign multiple values to the **author** column in the **BOOK** table, we need to expand our database's schema.

Let's do that by defining an **AUTHOR** table. It could include the following columns:

- Name

That may seem small, but let's start small and focus on getting the concept before going big.

With **AUTHOR** in place, we could insert a separate row for each of the authors just mentioned. We could also insert a row for Frank Herbert, Eric Carne, and Isaac Asimov as well.

But then comes the need to link that **author** with a **book**.

How?

We could add an additional column that references an entry in the **BOOK** table. But before we can do that, we need a unique reference for a given row in the **BOOK** table. And for that, we need a **key**.

WHAT IS A KEY?_

A **key** is simply a reference to a row of data in a given table. The simplest key would be an *integer*.

- Dune => 1
- Dune Messiah => 2
- Spring Data => 3

Each book in this BOOK table has a unique integer value associated with it. Simply put, we say that "1 is the key for *Dune* in the BOOK table. 2 is the key for *Dune Messiah* in the BOOK table."

By defining a unique value, we now have the means to reference a specific book from somewhere else in our database! Before we do that, we first need to give this new column a name. Since it identifies a unique identifying row, why not call it the **id** column?

NOTE: Some people prefer **id** without any aspect of its entity associated with it. In standard relational syntax (assuming the database itself is named LIBRARY), the column's full qualified name would be LIBRARY.BOOK.ID ({*database*}.{*table*}.{*column*}). Thus, it does have a strongly-scoped designation. Others like to imbue the column with a part of the entity and use something like **book_id**. Since we rarely use the fully qualified nomenclature, this also makes sense. Whatever your preference, be consistent in naming all your id columns using the same style.

It's important to understand that our table must also have some *constraints* applied to the **id** column to guarantee its unique identifying nature. What sort of properties are we talking?

Do you think it's safe to have two different rows holding the same **id** value? What about a row that has an empty **id** value? Does that even make sense?

No.

This is the reason that relational databases make it possible to specify the following characteristics on the **id** column:

- **PRIMARY KEY** - this alerts the database engine to treat the value as a *key*
- **UNIQUE** - database engine must ensure that any new value being inserted doesn't already exist
- **NOT NULL** - database engine ensures that any attempt to insert a new row *must* include a value for this column

If a row is inserted or updated in a way that violates one of the table's constraints, an error is thrown and the operation is aborted.

Many database engines provide **monotonic counters** through **sequence counters**. Monotonic counter is math-speak for "counter that only *increases* in value".

A sequence counter increments every time it's tapped, and

no two requests will ever give the *same* value to two different clients.

But monotonic counters are only recommended for traditional, monolithic database engines. Which may lead you to ask, why do monolithic database engines like sequence counters?

WHY DO MONOLITHIC DATABASE ENGINES LIKE SEQUENCE COUNTERS?_

Traditional database engines run in one location. Hence the term "monolithic". The entirety of their operation is contained in a single server.

You mitigate risks like server failures by having a *second* server running in hot standby mode *right next* to the primary. This secondary server typically has a synched up copy of every insert and update. Or in some configurations, the primary and the backup are both reading off the same disk array.

Whatever the configuration, they both live close together.

And all writes to the database are routed through whichever of these two servers is *active*.

Why?

It's the only way to guarantee that *all* inserts access the same monotonic sequence counter!

Mirror copies of the database can be distributed around the world, but these mirror copies are traditionally only for *reading*. Any and all *writes* must be routed to the primary server at the central facility.

Can you imagine if the primary server and all of its sequence counters were not in the same location?

A replicated server 5000 km away wants to do an insert, but it must ensure it's getting a unique, never-before-used primary key value. Any increments done on this remote server would have to communicate with the primary. This ensures that neither is dispensing an already-used key!

The latency cost of synching a sequence counter between these two servers would defeat the point of having distributed primary database servers!

Does requiring all writes go through a *single primary* server sound like a huge consequence for a simple sequence counter? How else would you guarantee getting the "next" integer in a sequence? Or is there some other way you could provide a guaranteed unique key? Some sort of **universally unique identification** generator?

WHY DO DISTRIBUTED DATABASE ENGINES LIKE UUIDS?_

Universally unique identifiers or **UUIDs** are a means to generate totally unique values (which we want) without having to talk to anyone else.

That means no need for a centrally located sequence counter to maintain its state. And with the requirement for a central sequence counter removed, the biggest requirement for routing all writes to a central server is gone!

Instead, we can focus on synching up new rows of data between distributed nodes, which even monolithic database engines with mirror replicas have to contend with.

Hence, a distributed database engine could have nodes running in every timezone around the world, and the only struggle they need to resolve is coordinating data changes.

Generating UUID values isn't free, but in this day and age, it isn't really a chore. But if you find yourself in a high-performance, large scale environment, there are ways to amortize that cost.

One tactic is to generate a hundred UUIDs up front and then hand them out as needed. Only when the supply dwindles down to a certain threshold do you need to generate another batch.

There are other approaches to generating unique keys, but we won't dig in.

The point is, that if we drop sequence counters in favor of another key-generating approach that is distributed-friendly, we can potentially move away from monolithic systems.

Whatever database engine you use, be it a monolithic or distributed one, we can instead focus our efforts on **managing related data**.

HOW DO WE MANAGE RELATED DATA?_

So we mentioned the need to have rows of BOOK data and rows of AUTHOR data. We mentioned the *Spring Data* book and its multiple authors. Imagine having this in our BOOK table:

- **`id`** `// title`
- **`3`** `// Spring Data`

With this in place, we could easily define some rows in an AUTHOR table:

- **`id`** `// name`
- **`1`** `// Mark Pollack`
- **`2`** `// Oliver Drotbohm`
- **`3`** `// Thomas Risberg`
- **`4`** `// Jonathon Brisbin`
- **`5`** `// Michael Hunger`

Notice that each AUTHOR entry *also* has a key?

If the BOOK table needs an **id** field, then doesn't it make sense for the AUTHOR table to have its own **id** column? And it should probably have the same constraints (PRIMARY KEY, UNIQUE, NOT NULL).

You could simply say that **book.id** and **author.id** are two *different* keys.

If you defined BOOK_SEQ and AUTHOR_SEQ to provide keys for BOOK and AUTHOR, it's vital that we don't *mix them up* in our application!

With this in mind, if we wanted to link a row in the AUTHOR table back to an entry in the BOOK table, all we need is an extra column, **book_id**:

- `id // name //` **`book_id`**
- `1 // Mark Pollack //` **`3`**
- `2 // Oliver Drotbohm //` **`3`**
- `3 // Thomas Risberg //` **`3`**
- `4 // Jonathon Brisbin //` **`3`**
- `5 // Michael Hunger //` **`3`**

That third column contains the **primary key** from the related BOOK table row "3". Looking at that listing, there are five authors (Pollack, Drotbohm, Risberg, Brisbin, and Hunger) associated with one book (*Spring Data*).

And that is how you link multiple rows in one table to a single row in another table!

The **book_id** column we just created is called a **foreign key**.

WHAT IS A FOREIGN KEY?_

A **foreign key** is a column in one table that references a **primary key** in *another* table.

The column name should clue you in that this is a reference to the BOOK table.

In fact it's a common convention to name such a column after the foreign table with a suffix of **_FK**. **book_fk** in this example.

Let's go back to *Dune* by Frank Herbert. What if we wanted to stock its sequel, *Dune Messiah*? Insert another row!

Our BOOK table should have the following data:

- **`id // title`**
- `1 // Dune - Frank Herbert`
- `2 // Dune Messiah - Frank Herbert`

However, our BOOK table doesn't have an **author** column anymore. We moved that information to the AUTHOR table to support multiple authors. That means our BOOK table should only contain this:

- id // **title**
- 1 // **Dune**
- 2 // **Dune Messiah**

And the AUTHOR table needs an entry for Frank Herbert, the author of the *Dune* franchise:

- id // name // **book_fk**
- 6 // Frank Herbert // **???**

Something wrong?

We inserted a row for Frank Herbert, but what do we put in the **book_fk** column? We can only store a single value, so what goes there?

Earlier we solved the problem of associating *one book* with *multiple authors*. That is called a **one-to-many relationship**.

In this situation we need to solve for *multiple books* having a *single author*. This is a **many-to-one relationship**.

We clearly need both, which is called a **many-to-many relationship**.

WHAT IS A MANY-TO-MANY RELATIONSHIP?_

When you have both a **one-to-many** and a **many-to-one** relationship between two tables, this is called a **many-to-many relationship**. A popular way to express this between the BOOK and the AUTHOR table is that "a book can have one or more authors, and an author can have one or more books."

Exactly how do we capture a many-to-many relationship, given we're confined to storing single values in columns?

What if we created a table called BOOK_AUTHOR and it had the following columns:

- **id**
- **book_fk**
- **author_fk**

It's not complicated. The **id** column is our handle on every given row. **book_fk** is a foreign key to the BOOK table. And **author_fk** is the foreign key to the AUTHOR table.

Now let's retool the AUTHOR table by dropping **book_fk**.

Since the BOOK table doesn't have any AUTHOR information, it would simply look like this:

- **id // title**
- 1 // Dune
- 2 // Dune Messiah

And this would be the AUTHOR table:

- **id // name**
- 6 // Frank Herbert

With all this information, we can now load the BOOK_AUTHOR table like this:

- **id // book_fk // author_fk**
- 1 // 1 // 6
- 2 // 2 // 6

The first row links *Dune* to Frank Herbert, and the second row links *Dune Messiah* to the same AUTHOR row. All in all, we can see two books, one author, and their linkage through the BOOK_AUTHOR table. In this situation, *two* books (ids 1 and 2) linked to *one* author (id 6)

What about the *Spring Data* book that we saw in prior chapters?

BOOK:

- **id** // title
- **3** // Spring Data

AUTHOR:

- **id** // name
- **1** // Mark Pollack
- **2** // Oliver Drotbohm
- **3** // Thomas Risberg
- **4** // Jonathon Bridbin
- **5** // Michael Hunger

BOOK_AUTHOR:

- id // **book_fk** // **author_fk**
- 3 // **3** // **1**
- 4 // **3** // **2**
- 5 // **3** // **3**
- 6 // **3** // **4**
- 7 // **3** // **5**

This shows *one* book (id 3) linked to *five* authors (ids 1, 2, 3, 4, 5)

Now we have a proper relationship between **books** and **authors**. We have multiple books and multiple authors. And we captured it in **multiple tables**.

WHY DO WE HAVE MULTIPLE TABLES?_

Hopefully you can see that by breaking up what at first seemed like *single* entries of data into *multiple* rows in *different* tables, and linking them together through **primary** and **foreign keys**, we have captured a proper relationship between various elements of our data.

This is **data analysis** and it must be done on anything we wish to store in a database. It's the only way to properly capture the schema of our data.

Newsflash: sometimes our initial data analysis will be wrong, and we won't realize it until after we're underway and using it in production.

That's okay.

It's possible that you started with a system that only had one author per book, but later on you realized it needs to be a **many-to-many** relationship.

Multiple tables with the right relationships between them also solves a different problem: making updates *efficiently*.

Let's imagine the BOOK table looked like this:

- **id // title**
- 1 // Dune
- 2 // Dune Messiah

AUTHOR table:

- **id // name**
- 6 // Frank Herberth

BOOK_AUTHOR:

- **id // book_fk // author_fk**
- 1 // 1 // 6
- 2 // 2 // 6

Do you notice anything wrong in our dataset? Perhaps a typo in Frank Herbert's name?? It's easy to fix. Simply issue the following update statement:

```
UPDATE author
SET name = 'Frank Herbert'
WHERE name = 'Frank Herberth'
```

That's pretty straight forward. In fact, this is incredibly efficient, because that copy of the author's name is only stored in *one place*.

What if we had never migrated the author's name into a separate AUTHOR table and instead kept it in the BOOK table?

- id // title // **author**
- 1 // Dune // **Frank Herberth**
- 2 // Dune Messiah // **Frank Herberth**

Now the typo is in *two* places. (How did that typo get there? Surely you've seen applications where the user enters one piece of data that is then copied elsewhere make mistakes like this!)

Of course we can write the same update:

```
UPDATE author
SET name = 'Frank Herbert'
WHERE name = 'Frank Herberth'
```

But it's important to understand that the database engine is now having to fix *two* rows of data. While not a deal breaker in and of itself, this potential for data duplication, if multiplied across the entire schema would introduce potential data consistency issues that may quickly become unmanageable!

Instead, it's better to properly model the relationships between the various bits of data and build relationships between tables that prevent such data inconsistency.

With separate BOOK and AUTHOR tables and a well-defined many-to-many relationship between them (through the BOOK_AUTHOR table), it would be much harder to enter an incorrect author name. And even if a bad entry were made, it wouldn't be hard to fix the data while maintaining data consistency.

In addition to the cost of making updates, is also the pure fact that storing an author's name twice (or over a hundred times for prolific writers like Isaac Asimov!) eats up disk space. While disk space shouldn't be a primary driver for decisions, it's a factor.

Redundant data takes up space and requires additional maintenance to ensure data integrity. The right structure with a proper relationship between tables reduces duplicate data and makes data maintenance as efficient as possible.

Up to this point, we've talked mostly about how to store

data and represent various relationships. But we haven't touched the good stuff: querying for data!

Querying is the whole reason we're doing this. What good is a database loaded with data if you never fetch any of it?

And having discovered a keen reason to spread our information across multiple tables, we are going to need to **join** our data to get it back!

WHAT IS A JOIN?_

Joining is what happens when you combine tables together to get a combination of information. For example in the previous chapters, we spent the time to properly represent a book with multiple authors, and an author with multiple books. That required putting the data into our BOOK table, the AUTHOR table, and the BOOK_AUTHOR table. This let us properly represent that **many-to-many relationship**.

Now if we want to answer the question "what is the title of every book and its author?" we need to fashion a **join**. Before we do that, let's imagine that our tables contain the following rows:

BOOK:

- **id // title**
- 1 // Dune
- 2 // Dune Messiah

AUTHOR:

- **id // name**
- 6 // Frank Herbert

BOOK_AUTHOR:

- **id // book_fk // author_fk**
- 1 // 1 // 6
- 2 // 2 // 6

The way to bring all this data back together is to write a SELECT statement with a JOIN, like this:

```
SELECT book.title, author.name
FROM book
JOIN book_author
ON book.id = book_author.book_fk
JOIN author
ON book_author.author_fk = author.id
```

The SELECT statement's "book.title, author.name" clause is called the **projection**. Those are the columns of data we are interested in fetching. You should note that it includes a column from the BOOK table as well as a column from the AUTHOR table. Specifically, we want the book's **title** and the author's **name**.

The first table where we can find some of this information is in the BOOK table. To reach it, we use the FROM clause.

But we don't stop there.

While it's true that the author's **name** is found in the AUTHOR table, we can't go directly from BOOK to AUTHOR. Because of our **many-to-many** relationship, we must first go *through* the BOOK_AUTHOR table. That means our next step is to **join** the BOOK table with the BOOK_AUTHOR table.

The point where these two tables match is the BOOK table's **id** column and the BOOK_AUTHOR table's **book_fk** column. This is accomplished with "JOIN book_author ON book.id = book_author.book_fk". The JOIN clause specifies what table we are joining into and the ON clause specifies the criteria applied.

Now that we've joined the BOOK_AUTHOR table, we are able to reach the AUTHOR table with one more **join**. To do that, we add "JOIN author ON book_author.author_fk = author.id". This works just like the previous join, connecting the AUTHOR table with a criteria that matches the BOOK_AUTHOR table's author_fk column with the AUTHOR table's id column.

Results:

- **`book.title // author.name`**
- `Dune // Frank Herbert`
- `Dune Messiah // Frank Herbert`

The two joins we just wrote are called **inner joins**. That means they are only applied if *both* sides of the ON clause's criteria exist and match. Another way to phrase is that both sides of the join are **required**.

There are other join types. The most common is an **outer join**. An outer join means something is **optional**.

How about an example?

What if you inserted a row into the BOOK table, but didn't know who its author was? It might look like this:

- **`id // title`**
- `4 // The Epic Of Gilgamesh`

The Epic Of Gilgamesh was written over 3,000 years ago,

and its author is unknown. Doesn't mean we can't have it in our library!

Because there is no associated author, there is nothing to insert into the AUTHOR table. That also means nothing in the BOOK_AUTHOR table.

If we ran the query we just pieced together earlier, this new book would *not* show up! When we write:

```
FROM book
JOIN book_author
ON book.id = book_author.book_fk
```

...we are saying we *only* want values that match on *both* sides. Hence, nothing in the results.

Since we just identified that AUTHOR should be **optional**, we must rewrite our query!

```
SELECT book.title, author.author
FROM book
LEFT OUTER JOIN book_author
ON book.id = book_author.book_fk
LEFT OUTER JOIN author
ON book_author.author_fk = author.id
```

Notice how each JOIN has turned into a LEFT OUTER JOIN? That carries some key aspects.

- LEFT includes all rows on the **left** hand side of the join.
- The **left** side of the join is the first table mentioned. (BOOK in this case).
- OUTER means that the rest is optional. In other words, grab all the rows on the left-hand side. If you can find a matching row on the right side, include its content. But if there's nothing, simply return NULL.

Running this new query, we can expect to see the following results:

- **`book.title // author.name`**
- `Dune // Frank Herbert`
- `Dune Messiah // Frank Herbert`
- `The Epic Of Gilgamesh //` *`NULL`*

WARNING: Because we are actually joining through TWO tables to get from BOOK to AUTHOR, both joins must be left outer. If we use an *inner join* on either, the row will get dropped.

We've discussed *left outer* joins quite a bit. Does that suggest there is a **right outer join**?

WHAT IS A RIGHT OUTER JOIN?_

We've talked about **inner joins** and **left outer joins**. Does this mean there might also be a **left join**, a **right join**, or a **right outer join**?

Yes!

For starters:

- LEFT JOIN is short for LEFT OUTER JOIN
- RIGHT JOIN is short for RIGHT OUTER JOIN
- JOIN is short for INNER JOIN

To clarify the language of join statements, it's important to understand that **LEFT** corresponds with the **first** table in any join clause. Remember this query from the previous chapter?

```
SELECT book.title, author.name
FROM book
LEFT OUTER JOIN book_author
ON book.id = book_author.book_fk
LEFT OUTER JOIN author
ON book_author.author_fk = author.id
```

When you have "FROM book LEFT OUTER JOIN

book_author", BOOK is the **left** portion of the first join, and BOOK_AUTHOR is on the **right**. You could also say the BOOK table is joining into the BOOK_AUTHOR table from the left-hand side.

In the second join of that query, BOOK_AUTHOR is now on the **left** and AUTHOR is on the **right**. In that situation, BOOK_AUTHOR is joining into the AUTHOR table from the left-hand side.

We commonly read queries from top to bottom. And there are exceptions.

Because a left outer join always brings in all values from the left, i.e. the "top", while the values on the right are optional, it's easy to see left outer joins as being "top required" and "bottom optional".

Looking at the query above, it says that BOOK rows are required, but BOOK_AUTHOR rows are optional. And reading a top-to-bottom paradigm as required/optional is quite conventional with many ways that we perceive things. For example, clicking an element at the top of a UI can *optionally* show detailed information below it.

A *right outer join* flips that on its head.

Because the **right** side of the join is on the "bottom", a right outer join would mean top/bottom is optional/required.

Huh? If that confused you, go back and re-read that paragraph again.

It's important to point out that if you swap the order of things, a left outer join can rewritten as a right outer join.

```
SELECT book.title, author.name
FROM author
RIGHT OUTER JOIN book_author
ON author.id = book_author.author_fk
RIGHT OUTER JOIN book
ON book_author.book_fk = book.id
```

This query means the *exact same thing* as the previous one. Even though it looks like it was twisted inside out, it will produce the same results. AUTHOR is joined with BOOK_AUTHOR, but because it's a **right outer join**, the BOOK_AUTHOR rows will be matched against optional AUTHOR rows. But don't overlook the fact that BOOK_AUTHOR is right outer joined with BOOK, meaning all BOOK rows will be matched with optional BOOK_AUTHOR rows. This makes AUTHOR and BOOK_AUTHOR *optional*, while the BOOK rows are *required*.

This is why you'll tend to see enterprises favor *left outer joins* over *right outer joins*.

This example of right outer joins pushes us to read the query starting at the bottom, which goes against the grain. We're used to reading things from the top.

But this isn't simply because our native tongue probably reads from the top of the page.

The projection of the SELECT clause is always at the top. Reading the project at the top and then jumping to the bottom to read all the joins requires us to do a lot of mental skipping to hold that all together.

Also consider the fact that this example query is relatively short. What if we were dealing with a three-page query?

I did see one example of someone using a right outer join, but that involved a query that had already been developed that was quite extensive. Most of the query used left outer joins. But later in the development of that query, after much work had been invested in it, the OP discovered they needed one additional join to get a required field. Instead of attempting to rewrite the whole thing from scratch, they simply tacked the additional join at the end.

There are situations that need right outer joins, but they tend to be the exception.

Perhaps this convinces you to prefer *left outer joins* over *right outer joins*, but what about LEFT OUTER JOIN versus just LEFT JOIN? After all, they mean the same thing, right?

For me, the OUTER token helps me "see" that this is an outer join faster and that the table we're going into is *optional*.

It's the same reason I prefer simply using using JOIN instead of INNER JOIN. One less token for me to visually parse. If I saw LEFT JOIN and INNER JOIN all over the code, the coherence between the two is diminished. There are two tokens in every join, so I must hone in the first token to discriminate. Additionally, one is four characters long while the other is five. That further slows my visual parsing ability. Yes, one of them starts with "L" and the other with "I", both even those letters look quite similar.

However, if I see JOIN and LEFT OUTER JOIN everywhere, then I can quickly see the singular JOIN token and quickly spot this as an inner join that's required. When I see LEFT OUTER JOIN, the LEFT OUTER tokens serve as a qualifier that my brain turns into *optional*. And I'm done.

Maybe that sounds confusing? Maybe not.

This was actually a style I learned from someone that had been doing database design for years before me. And after ten years of reading queries on that contract, this standard became easy to visually parse.

- JOIN = inner, *required* values
- LEFT OUTER JOIN = outer, *optional* values

And to be honest, after writing over two hundred queries, I never once wrote a *right outer join*, if that helps.

To round out the subject of various types of joins, I want to share that there is also a FULL OUTER JOIN. It's still an outer join in that optional rows are brought in.

FULL means that results aren't confined to LEFT or RIGHT. Instead, this join will bring in *all* rows from *both* sides of the join.

The values from the left side ("top") are optional, but so are the values from the right side ("bottom") as well. Basically, both sides are optional, a situation I struggle to find a meaningful example.

Online examples I've seen combine CUSTOMER data with ORDERS. This means that if you have customers *without* orders as well as orders *without* customers, a FULL OUTER JOIN would show you both, all at once. But can you imagine a real world situation where this would happen?

I have never written a **full outer join** to solve a problem nor stumbled across a scenario where neither JOIN nor LEFT OUTER JOIN didn't offer what I needed. And I have yet to meet anyone with such a problem. Do you have a query that fits that? Message me if you do.

Writing queries and joining multiple tables, each filled with perhaps millions or even billions of rows and producing a practical result set, requires that you understand the **cartesian product**.

WHAT IS A CARTESIAN PRODUCT?

The last time you may have heard the word **cartesian** was possibly in algebra class, when you encountered **cartesian coordinates**.

Named after French mathematician René Descartes, cartesian coordinates describe every combination of X-values paired with Y-values. For example, if the X-axis has 1, 2, 3, 4, and so on, and the Y-axis has the same, the coordinates of a cartesian coordinate grid would be captured by combining them like this:

- `(X-axis value, Y-axis value)`
- `(1, 1)`
- `(2, 1)`
- `(3, 1)`
- `(4, 1)`
- `(1, 2)`
- `(2, 2)`
- `(3, 2)`
- `(4, 2)`
- `(1, 3)`
- …

To keep this simple, let's go back to when we had each BOOK associated with one author linked by a **book_fk** in the AUTHOR table.

Now swap out the X-axis values with these book entries:

- **id // title**
- 1 // Dune
- 3 // Spring Data
- 4 // The Epic of Gilgamesh

And exchange the Y-axis values with these author entries:

- **id // name // book_fk**
- 1 // Frank Herbert // 1
- 2 // Mark Pollack // 3

The cartesian coordinates expansion would look a little like this:

- **(book entry, author entry)**
- (1 // Dune, 1 // Frank Herbert // 1)
- (3 // Spring Data, 1 // Frank Herbert // 1)
- (4 // The Epic of Gilgamesh, 1 // Frank Herbert // 1)
- (NULL, 1 // Frank Herbert // 1)
- (1 // Dune, 2 // Mark Pollack // 3)
- (3 // Spring Data, 2 // Mark Pollack // 3)
- (4 // The Epic of Gilgamesh, 2 // Mark Pollack // 3)
- (NULL, 2 // Mark Pollack // 3)
- (1 // Dune, NULL)

- (3 // Spring Data, NULL)
- (4 // The Epic Of Gilgamesh, NULL)
- (NULL, NULL)

This is the **cartesian product**.

In case you're confused about the entries with NULL, just think of them as the "o" coordinate in relational databases.

The point is that by combining every possible BOOK with every possible AUTHOR, we get a complete matrix of combinations. This is what a join does before you apply the ON clause!

You might have a hunch as to what the ON clause does. If you guessed filtering out un-matched combinations of the **cartesian product**, you go to the head of the class.

If we were to write:

```
SELECT book.title, author.name
FROM book
JOIN author
ON book.id = author.book_fk
```

...we should expect this:

- **(book entry, author entry)**
- (**1** // Dune, 1 // Frank Herbert // **1**)
- ~~(3 // Spring Data, 1 // Frank Herbert // 1)~~
- ~~(4 // The Epic of Gilgamesh, 1 // Frank Herbert // 1)~~
- ~~(NULL, 1 // Frank Herbert // 1)~~
- ~~(1 // Dune, 2 // Mark Pollack // 3)~~
- (**3** // Spring Data, 2 // Mark Pollack // **3**)
- ~~(4 // The Epic of Gilgamesh, 2 // Mark Pollack // 3)~~

- ~~`(NULL, 2 // Mark Pollack // 3)`~~
- ~~`(1 // Dune, NULL)`~~
- ~~`(3 // Spring Data, NULL)`~~
- ~~`(4 // The Epic Of Gilgamesh, NULL)`~~
- ~~`(NULL, NULL)`~~

First of all, we have the exact same pairs of values we saw before. That's because we're joining the exact same tables with the exact same values.

However the ON clause in the join causes the rows where **book.id** (furthest value to the left) and **author.book_fk** (furthest value to the right) don't match to get filtered out. And because this is an *inner* join, the NULL rows are also cut.

In this case, ten out of twelve rows are dropped from the final results.

And this only joined two tables. In the chapter where we talked about a many-to-many relationship that involved three tables, we encounter the same thing. The only difference is that instead of a 2-D matrix as shown above, imagine a 3-D combination of values, with each axis (X, Y, and Z) mapping onto each table's values (BOOK, BOOK_AUTHOR, and AUTHOR).

This is where it's vital to point out that the database engine can actually *rearrange* the order it carries out our joins. It can choose to join either BOOK with BOOK_AUTHOR or BOOK_AUTHOR with AUTHOR first. The order doesn't matter.

There is a word that describes this property: **commutative**. It's the same property that says that 1+2 = 2+1.

And this is why every database engine on the planet invests huge resources in building **optimizers** that can analyze and figure out *which* join most efficiently produces the *smallest* results.

The smaller the result of generating the **cartesian product** and filtering non-matching rows, the faster the next join will be due to the reduced volume of rows that must be matched.

This is also why we must understand when left outer join is needed and when it's not.

When we perform a left outer join, we're pulling in more rows. To overuse it and then "filter out" later, perhaps in your application instead of inside the database engine, means you're wasting the database engine's ability to filter on your behalf.

And database engines are *great* at filtering!

The more you can push things onto the database engine, the better.

Another way to phrase this is that database engines are great at filtering out rows of data, because they are also great at deciding *what* to filter first!

WHAT IS A QUERY FILTER?_

If you're not careful, the database can knock your application on its head. Consider a query like this:

```
SELECT *
FROM book
```

That query will cause the whole table to get handed back to you.

Maybe this is no big deal when dealing with an example database like we've been dabbling with here. After all, what's five rows more or less?

But what if your BOOK table has 1,000,000 rows? 10,000,000 rows? A billion rows?

Hence the need to add a **query filter**!

```
SELECT *
FROM book
WHERE title = 'The Epic Of Gilgamesh'
```

That simple WHERE clause *filters* your query results. It's also possible to combine multiple query filters as well.

```
SELECT *
FROM book
WHERE title = 'The Epic of Gilgamesh'
```

```
OR title = 'Dune'
```

A query filter can be appended to any query (and it's often recommended). Check it out!

```
SELECT book.title, author.name
FROM book
LEFT OUTER JOIN book_author
ON book.id = book_author.book_fk
LEFT OUTER JOIN author
ON author.id = book_author.author_fk
WHERE author.name = 'Mark Pollack'
OR author.name = 'Frank Herbert'
```

The gift of writing queries involves:

- **Joining** the right **tables**
- Applying the right **query filters**
- And then selecting the relevant **columns**

That's not complicated. But it does require understanding the semantic relationship between tables.

For example, what if you wrote that previous SELECT but didn't make them *left outer* joins? With such a relatively simple *many-to-many* relationship between two entities (BOOK and AUTHOR), we've already seen reasons to use both *inner* joins as well as *left outer* joins.

Imagine writing a report that demands joining **twenty different** tables.

Having learned what **cartesian products** are, how **joins** work, and how to apply **query filters**, it may feel a bit overwhelming to comprehend how database engines can do all this brute force work.

But let's look a little closer and think about finding a single book. Do you know how a database engine looks in the AUTHOR table and finds books written by **Frank Herbert**?

You may think that the database engine simply scans through the entire AUTHOR table and looks for every row that matches. But as mentioned early in this chapter, what if you had a huge database? What if that database stored 10 MM books and 5 MM authors? Can you imagine scanning all 5 MM rows of the AUTHOR table every time you needed a single book?

As a visual example, my master's thesis is published at the Auburn University library, a facility that is five stories tall. Finding my thesis would entail visiting every book on every shelf of every stack on every floor.

How efficient is that?

This is why we need **indexes**.

Let's go back to finding that book at the university library in a five-story facility. Wouldn't it be nice if there was a record somewhere that said "Greg's Thesis => 3rd floor, second stack, fifth shelf, 3rd from the end"?

Maybe you're old enough to remember the library's card catalog? (Maybe you're not!)

In the olden days, the card catalog was just a small box of cards with the coordinates for every book. It's like taking every book in the building, and boiling it down to two pieces of information: the attribute your searching for (*title*) and it's location.

Card catalogs typically had more than one set of cards. The first set would be based on *title*. The second set was based on *author*. And one other key aspect of a card catalog is that it's sorted on the attribute you're looking up (*title* or *author*). Because the card catalog is sorted, you can find an entry quickly, and then it tells you where the book is.

That is what an **index** is!

For a given table of information, you can build any number of indexes based on the attributes you need to find things.

Imagine our library with 10 MM books. People often search on *title*. So a keen index to setup would be based on *title*.

```
CREATE INDEX ON book (title)
```

This will create a "card catalog" inside the database that has the *title* of every book in it. And that index is sorted by *title*.

And what's in the index when you find the entry? The actual location of the row of the BOOK table with that title.

With that information, the database engine can jump straight to it.

This works whether we're talking about some monolithic database where the blocks of that row are on the same server, or on a distributed database and the row you seek is on the other side of the globe.

When you type:

```
SELECT *
FROM book
WHERE title = 'Spring Data'
```

...the database engine is able to quickly find the entry for *Spring Data* in the index in logarithmic time. Then the index entry will tell it exactly where that row of data is.

As your database grows in size, indexes become paramount in finding data. In fact, indexes are one of the most performative things you can apply to your database.

Imagine a database with 10 MM books and no indexes. What does it mean to do that query you just saw?

It would require a **full table scan**. That literally means scanning every single row.

That ain't cheap.

But with a single statement you create an index based on *title*. And run the query again.

The database engine will then scan your newly minted index to find the entry.

Remember, the index is sorted. The database engine jumps

to the middle. From there, it figures out if it overshot. If it did, then it throws away the upper half. Otherwise, it throws away the lower half. Rinse and repeat.

With 10 MM rows, the database engine can find the entry in twenty four hops or less. Instead of checking 10 MM rows, it instead just needs to check twenty four. This is a binary search, and it's only possible in a sorted collection.

Indexes provide sorted subsets of your data allowing search efficiency to scale by an exponential amount. This is the reason many blurt out "create an index!" when anyone asks "how can I speed this query up?"

It's also the reason you can actually hinder things when creating the wrong indexes.

Remember that card catalog? A separate, boiled-down "copy" of the database that is sorted for your benefit?

Think of an index as a secondary database that the engine maintains on your behalf. What happens to an index when you add another book to the inventory?

Not only is it added to the BOOK table. It must *also* be added to the index. And it must be put in order just like the other entries.

If we're talking about a single new book that's not a problem. But what if we're talking about 100,000 new books?

In addition to inserting the same rows into the BOOK table as before, you must also add 100,000 new entries to that index. And those new entries must be sorted.

It's certainly possible. Just sort the incoming dataset by *title* and then do an insertion sort. But it's certainly not free. There is a cost.

And once the job is complete, the query we used earlier but looking for one of those new titles would look like this:

```
SELECT *
FROM book
```

```
WHERE title = 'Spring Data - 2024 Edition'
```

And it will soar. Probably in sub-second time.

Is this the only hindrance that comes with indexes?

Unfortunately, no.

Indexes sizzle when someone asks for **one** book. The index quickly tells you where it lives. And that's awesome.

But what happens when you're looking for a bigger result set? Imagine something like "find every folio in the library and flag it for audit".

Folios are uniquely formatted books. This includes oversized books, microfiche, and other odd types that don't fit on regular book shelves. As a consequence, a library's inventory of folios must be audited periodically to ensure they're available for checkout, or they can be scheduled for repair or replacement.

If you were the director of the library and you wanted to schedule such an audit, you need to know all the books that are in this format. And so you'd write something like this:

```
SELECT *
FROM book
WHERE format = 'folio'
```

In a library with 10 MM books that has an index based on *format*, instead of giving you a single entry in that index that you visit **once**, you may instead get **100,000 entries**.

That may only be 1% of your inventory. But imagine using an index the way we just did earlier. Basically, you're visiting the card catalog, finding a stack of entries, and then having to visit the actual books amidst the library 100,000 times!

What if the query you wrote hit 10% of all entries? 40%? 80%?

At a certain point, it's actually *faster* and *more efficient* to sidestep the index and simply visit every book in the library. Going to the index, getting a subset of books, and then visiting every entry, may actually be *slower* than a full table scan.

This is where I'd like to mention that there are actually different types of indexes. One of them is known as a covering index. This is an index that doesn't just have the search criteria sorted. It also has additional columns stored in the index as well. This means that your entire query could be served by the index and not even need to go to the table.

There are all kinds of tradeoffs when you do this. For example, would you want to put *all* the columns into a covering index? That requires a lot of disk space and an increased amount of I/O to maintain it.

This is just some of the tidbits concerning one type of index. There are actually many types of indexes and out of scope of this book.

The point is that the old adage of "just create an index!" can sometimes be **wrong**.

I've said it before, rules of thumb work until they don't.

We can build all kinds of indexes to help with queries. But on occasion, we need to signal that we've done enough research and for *this* query, we do *not* want to use the index.

And this is exactly what **query hints** are for!

WHAT IS A QUERY HINT?_

A query hint is something that is used to nudge the database engine's query optimizer to pick a different path.

Query optimizer?

Different path?

What are you talking about??

The previous chapter discussed what indexes are and how they can improve query performance by leaps and bounds. But it's important to understand that indexes are just one component of the database engine's overall process for servicing your query request.

To discuss the entire process, we need to zoom out a little.

Every database engine on the planet has an optimizer to assist in the handling of queries. Basically, it's the database engine's algorithm that attempts to take your declarative SQL query and transform it into the most efficient thing possible.

For example, if your query joins three tables, there is no requirement that it complete the first declared join first. It may be more favorable to start with the *last* join. Queries, fundamentally, are commutative operations, meaning that no matter which order you carry them out, the results will be the same. Commutative is the concept that 1+2 = 2+1. For join statements this is applicable. (Just so you know, there are other situations where the commutative principle does not apply.)

Simply put, the faster you can "throw away" rows of irrelevant data and shrink a given result set, the better.

Perhaps an example is in order? Imagine a query like this:

```
SELECT book.title, author.name
FROM book
LEFT OUTER JOIN book_author
ON book.id = book_author.book_fk
LEFT OUTER JOIN  author
ON author.id = book_author.author_fk
WHERE author.name = 'Mark Pollack'
```

The database engine gets to choose the order it joins the tables. If you joined all BOOK entries with the BOOK_AUTHOR table, you'd have an intermediate result set. It pretty much looks like any other table in that it has rows of data with a distinct set of columns. (If you're confused by this, go back to **What is a cartesian product?**)

That intermediate result set is then joined with the AUTHOR table, producing a final result set with a complete representation of the BOOK-to-AUTHOR relationship. And then the engine can filter on the AUTHOR.NAME column.

In a database with 10 MM books and 5 MM authors, if you're visualizing a *huge* intermediate result set being put together to filter for *one* author, you would be right!

What if the engine started with the AUTHOR table? And before it entertains the first LEFT OUTER JOIN, it instead applied the query filter **author.name = 'Mark Pollack'**? The entire AUTHOR table would be shrunk down to a single row.

5 MM authors flanged down to one.

And even though this is a row of a table, in this context, this single row is an intermediate result set that is partially fulfilling the query.

What if the database engine then takes that intermediate result set and does a LEFT OUTER JOIN with the BOOK_AUTHOR table?

That, too, would naturally produce a relatively small secondary result set. After all, it's only looking for instances of the BOOK_AUTHOR table that reference that one author.

Finally, join that intermediate result set with the BOOK table, and you can probably visualize a very *fast* result set.

A result set that has the *same* result as the first way we talked about earlier.

Now do you see why the database engine wants to "throw away rows" as fast as possible to speed things up?

The little algorithm that decided to change the order is what every database engine calls its **optimizer**.

With that basic understanding, it's not hard to imagine more complex and detailed queries.

For example, what if you had multiple query filter criteria spread across the various tables? Simple filter criteria like AND clauses can scale easily.

The optimizer could iterate across every filter criteria and apply each one to its respective table first in order to shrink down those tables into smaller intermediate result sets. From there, it could then start carrying out joins.

Maybe it stands out, maybe it doesn't, but as a general guide you start with the smallest sized table and join from there. But other factors can kick in.

All this to say that database optimizers are powerful and will look at your data and your query to pick the most efficient path.

This is why it's so important to embed as *much semantic*

information as possible into your database tables. And to also grant the queries as much information as possible as well.

It's possible to do stuff outside the database engine, but there's an inherent risk to that. For example, the query above could instead have been done like this:

```
SELECT book.title, author.name
FROM book
LEFT OUTER JOIN book_author
ON book.id = book_author.book_fk
LEFT OUTER JOIN  author
ON author.id = book_author.author_fk
```

This is the same query as before, but without the author name criteria applied. Instead, this result set could be handed back to the application, and the application does the filtering.

That would still produce the same results.

But that would be a *huge* mistake.

You are hiding from the database engine that you want to filter by **author.name**. If you share that additional criteria with the engine, it will avoid loading up 10 MM rows x 5 MM rows. Instead, by giving the database engine *all* of your criteria, it can do a much more effective job of finding the answer.

Sometimes we imagine getting back an intermediate result set, and then wanting to let the user enter filtering criteria in the UI. But managing such a ginormous intermediate result set is probably not the best idea.

Instead, take the user's inputs, send them over the wire to the database, re-running the query each time, and taking the results back to the UI. Even as each character is typed. The user enters "M", the query is run. The user enters "a", the query is run again. The user enters "r" and "k", each time the query is run again.

Even though this sounds worse, in truth, it will probably perform better.

That's because you would remove *any* situation in which you are asking for the *entire* result set of all books and their authors being queried and sent over the wire.

And if you institute a 500ms delay before sending the user's currently typed filter over the wire, you would probably achieve a suitable balance between UI and database engine power.

Lean into the optimizer and try not to outthink it. It probably knows more about the data than you!

But we started this section talking about **query hints**. So what are they?

Query hints are ways to "nudge" the database engine in a certain direction. For starters, query hints are database engine specific. Some are as simple as "use this index instead of what you think you should use," or "do NOT use this index even if you want to."

There are other query hints for different database engines that instructs it on various ways of caching or bypassing caches. Some query hints are work arounds for current bugs, which means that at some point in the future, that query hint may no longer even have any effect.

One thing should be clear...a query hint is a *suggestion* not an **ultimatum**. You have to read the docs for your specific database engine to understand how much force a given query hint has.

That's why it's good to *not* overuse query hints!

Instead of putting hints into too many queries, and repeatedly attempt to override the optimizer, it is a better investment of your time and energy to build indexes that best serve your queries.

It should be on rare occasion that you need to override the optimizer. In fact, the only time to consider query hints, if at all, should only be after you've rewritten a query, analyzed it, and inspected the indexes you developed to serve your needs.

After all, the whole point of using a relational database is to gather information and structure it in a proper format, representing the semantics of your domain model. Also, the goal is to have properly normalized data, such that the optimizer can properly throw away the “right” bits of data when filtering and joining.

Which raises the question, what is normalized data?

WHAT IS NORMALIZED DATA?_

So far, we have talked about how the need to store various types of data leads to multiple tables. And we have seen **one-to-many** relationships between data.

For example, one author can write many books.

We also saw how a one-to-many relationship between two entities becomes a **many-to-many** relationship. For example, a book can have multiple authors, and an author can have multiple books.

With single-valued rows of data in tables, and single-valued elements in each column, the need to use one-to-many relationships became our solution for these more complex relationships.

But there is a more subtle thing that arises when we work with data in this manner: **Data normalization**. Data normalization is when we find the most efficient means of storing the underlying semantic knowledge.

If all we had was a single table with infinite rows and columns, we could model our library system kind of like this:

- **`title // author`**

- Dune // Frank Herbert
- Dune Messiah // Frank Herbert
- Spring Data // Mark Pollack
- Spring Data // Oliver Drotbohm
- Spring Data // Thomas Risberg

That's pretty straight forward in capturing ALL the information at hand. We have every book's title, and we have every author's name. And we can also see how each author is related to each book.

But do you notice anything wrong? Or at least, anything that is not preferable? There is a lot of duplication. We can see Frank Herbert listed **twice**. The *Spring Data* book, while each author is only listed once, is itself shown **three** times.

There is a lot of duplicate content when we put *all* the data into one big table!

At a glance, it may not seem hard to find a given book. Just write something like this:

```
SELECT *
FROM BIG_TABLE
WHERE title = 'Dune'
```

That would give us back:

- Frank Herbert // Dune

That looks alright, yeah?

But what happens if we alter the parameter to 'Spring Data', but change nothing else?

```
SELECT *
FROM BIG_TABLE
WHERE title = 'Spring Data'
```

- Mark Pollack // Spring Data

- Oliver Drotbohm // Spring Data
- Thomas Risberg // Spring Data

Now what? Is this right? Is it wrong?

The correct answer is: it depends!

This is an ambiguous result set, because the table in and of itself doesn't tell us if it's a BOOK table or an AUTHOR table. How should this map into our object structure in our application? One book with an embedded list of three authors? Three author entries each with a copy of the book entry?

The database itself doesn't know nor tell us, because this table is literally an *entire database stored in one table.*

Since we requested **SELECT ***, we literally asked for everything the database had to offer. What we make of it is our problem.

So let's refine our request a bit. What if we asked "Who wrote *Dune*?"

```
SELECT author_name
FROM BIG_TABLE
WHERE title = 'Dune'
```

- Frank Herbert

That's straightforward.

"Who wrote *Spring Data*?"

```
SELECT author_name
FROM BIG_TABLE
WHERE title = 'Spring Data'
```

- Mark Pollack
- Oliver Drotbohm
- Thomas Risberg

Still looking alright. How far can we go with this?

"What books did Frank Herbert write?"

```
SELECT title
FROM BIG_TABLE
WHERE author_name = 'Frank Herbert'
```

- Dune
- Dune Messiah

That's three for three.

Let's cut to the chase, is there a limit on how far querying one BIG_TABLE is vs. a database where the tables are split up into BOOK, AUTHOR, and BOOK_AUTHOR like we had before?

The answer is an emphatic *no*. There is *no* limit to querying such a table.

You see, this BIG_TABLE is fundamentally what you get when you join together BOOK, AUTHOR, and BOOK_AUTHOR based upon their relationships to each other. The intermediate result set from which the query filter is applied is the same thing!

So what's the deal? Why go to all this trouble to split things up when we could just do this??

Remember the duplication issue? We briefly mentioned it, but didn't delve too deeply into it.

Maybe this is the time to bring up a little fact...Frank Herbert wrote over twenty books. But that's just scratching the surface. C.S. Lewis wrote almost forty books. And Isaac Asimov, one of the most prolific authors of the 20th Century, wrote over five hundred books. In these examples, we are only seeing two rows for Frank Herbert.

Imagine storing the textual value of "Isaac Asimov" five hundred times in a database. That string is 12 characters long, counting the space in the middle. It would take 6000 bytes to store a 12-byte string that many times!

Of course, disk storage is one of the lowest-cost commodities in modern computing. So it can't be purely disk consumption that's at stake. And it's not.

What if you needed to update that value in the database? Isaac Asimov passed away in 1992. But imagine a modern-day author that was loaded into our library. What if our database tracked the date of their birth and their death, and we needed to make an update? Imagine updating 500+ records to ensure they are ALL correct.

Not only is that expensive, but there is an inherent risk of not completing the operation. How would we compensate for an update that somehow only updated 499 out of the 500 entries? The next query for that particular author might return the wrong answer.

This is what leads us to wanting to store every piece of information in a database *once* and *only once*. The names "Isaac Asimov", "Frank Herbert", "Greg L. Turnquist', "Mark Pollack", "Oliver Drotbohm", and "Thomas Risberg" should be stored once and only once in our database.

That way, any update only has to be **once**. And here we see the ultimate engineering tradeoff:

> We can either speed up queries by having everything joined in one big table...or we can reduce duplication and risk of consistency and have everything stored once!

To zoom out a bit, remember our 10 MM row BOOK and 5 MM row AUTHOR database representing our library? Imagine merging those tables into one Big Table. At a minimum, the total thing would be AT LEAST 10 MM rows (one for each title). It will certainly be more than that due to multiple authors.

And more importantly, that big database would have *many more columns*. Basically ***columns(BOOK)*** + ***columns(AUTHOR)***.

When you structure your data such that you have no duplicate content, occupying the **minimum** amount of space possible, and only using **foreign keys** to link tables together, this is known as **3rd Normal Form** or **3NF**.

This is what the industry calls normalized data.

With normalized data, you have taken the time to identify the exact relationship between the various entities. This relationship between various entities can be a complex process. There are times when you may map things one-to-one and later discover the need to change that relationship to one-to-many.

Another relationship may be seen as one-to-many but later evolves to many-to-many.

We've already seen that different relationships beg for different types of joins. Simply moving from one-to-many to many-to-many requires bringing in an intermediate table. This isn't hard, but it isn't trivial either.

And the joins needed to navigate through these relationships change.

Perhaps you're thinking "why not just make *everything* many-to-many and go from there?"

While noble, that would require putting an intermediate table between every single entity table in the schema. We've already seen how we had to move from:

```
SELECT book.title, author.name
FROM book
JOIN author
ON book.author_fk = author.id
```

to

```
SELECT book.title, author.name
FROM book
JOIN book_author
ON book.id = book_author.book_fk
JOIN author
ON author.id = book_author.author_fk
```

to

```
SELECT book.title, author.name
FROM book
LEFT OUTER JOIN book_author
ON book.id = book_author.book_fk
LEFT OUTER  JOIN author
ON author.id = book_author.author_fk
```

Making everything many-to-many and optional dials up the verbosity and complexity of the whole structure. It's also important to recognize that the more tables you have, the more costly the storage. It also increases the maintenance and performative costs of proper indexes.

Instead, it's best to capture the true relationship of your data to the best of your ability and then let your data grow naturally over time. Which leads to another question, what happens when data grows and grows and grows?

WHAT HAPPENS WHEN DATA GROWS AND GROWS AND GROWS?_

One of the biggest surprises when it comes to databases is how dynamic it all is. And not just in one way. But in fact, many ways, things will change to your astonishment.

How about an example?

I worked on a contract that started back in 2001. We were building a nation-wide communications network, working with all the various telecommunications providers big and small. And this required that we monitor all the equipment at all the sites so we could detect an outage.

The rollout on the contract was to start with twenty two sites. Twenty two sites with a couple hundred services is hardly anything at all. And that's a good thing. We needed to get warmed up on building these services as well as monitoring them.

We worked out what the various entity types were and how they were related to each other. What's a device? What's a card? Does every device even have cards? No? Okay. What about ports? Some alarms are reported at the device level, some at the port level. Some devices have ports and some have cards that have their own ports.

It took a few months, but we had something operational. And this included writing a fistful of queries so the monitoring application I was responsible for could see an incoming SNMP alarm and correlate it with the device that had failed. We'd open a ticket and alert the operations staff so they could then start their process for effecting repairs.

The part that's not mentioned in this example is that twenty two sites with a couple hundred devices would eventually scale over the next two years to eight thousand sites with closer to three hundred thousand devices.

At that point in time, queries I had written two years ago didn't scale.

Read that one again: queries I had written two years ago **did not scale**.

What's a real world instance where something that worked at first failed later?

Hostname resolution is consider case insensitive. Every alarm that flowed into our system included a hostname. But the case was mixed. Some would be all caps, some lowercase. But the table that contained all the hostnames only had one entry for that device.

So we said early on, "Just apply an upper() function on each side when you apply a query filter!" And yes, that solved the problem. Any hostname on the alarm would properly match the hostname in the related table.

What we didn't know was that using an upper() function was causing us to sidestep the index. The hostnames were indexed, but not the uppercase version of the hostnames. Hence, every query that did that resulted in a full table scan. Re-read **What is an index?** if you need a refresher.

A table that grows from two hundred entries to three hundred thousand entries results in a 1500x increase in cost!

Those queries may have been sub-second when I first wrote them, but now they were taking seconds.

To further compound the problem, not only did the queries take longer to run due to the roughly 1500x increase in equipment, but the volume of alarm data that flowed into the data center increased by a similar amount.

So imagine a 1500x increase multiplied by a 1500x increase in traffic that has to be correlated that way.

Back of the envelope calculation will show this to a 1 MM-fold increase in cost.

My queries from two years earlier **did not scale**.

Thankfully, that team had a devoted Database Administrator (DBA) assigned to us. He helped us analyze and rewrite queries. He taught me so much. The most valuable being how to use EXPLAIN PLAN to grok what the database is up to for a given query.

Every database comes with a certain version of EXPLAIN PLAN. However, it's not a standard, so they are all different. But fundamentally, you type EXPLAIN {SQL statement}, and the database engine spits out an analysis of your query instead of the results. (Some will do both).

And that report will typically show you what the engine did first, how many rows it took to do it, whether or not indexes were used, and how many rows of every phase were involved. The query I mentioned earlier reported *multiple* **full table scans**.

And as mentioned in **What is an index?**, full table scans are *bad*.

So I got to work. I had to rewrite multiple queries. I had to consider not just that aspect of case insensitivity, but also the relationship between various tables.

Some tables may have a 1-to-many relationship, but if the

"many" table in that situation has only like four rows because it represents an enumerated constant that won't be changing much over time, then there is little to be gained in optimizing that join.

However, two tables that each have hundreds of thousands of rows and are also in a 1-to-many relationship may require more attention. That's why it's vital to find out which queries are eating up the database engine's time the most and focus on them first.

I have seen database engines that have something called TopSQL, a tool like "top" that will show you which queries are eating up the most time.

I had learned of TopSQL because that contract reached a point a few years later where the database was hitting 100% CPU utilization on a daily basis around noon.

They had assembled a strategic team to divine what was happening and how to deal it. I was not a part of that team, but happened to be walking by one of their meetings and peeked at the overhead. They were focused on query #1. I spotted that query #2 was mine, and from a different application that had nothing to do with network monitoring.

I asked some questions and realized that a business office application that wasn't "mission critical" was in fact incredibly inefficient and eating up ridiculous amounts of CPU time.

The original developer of that app had rolled off the contract, and I had inherited his app. I dug and uncovered a query that took twenty minutes to run.

Yup. Twenty minutes.

This app had been out there for years to help the business office provision new sites. But because it wasn't "mission critical" it had received little priority.

I found the query that was eating up so many resources and

ran it through EXPLAIN PLAN. And I discovered that it was joining the same table twenty times. Twenty times.

Not because there was a semantic reason to.

No.

The query was grabbing various views that had parts of information that application needed and stitching it all together.

In case you didn't know, reaching for someone else's database view is a big no-no for precisely this reason.

Anytime you draw up a new query, you should start with joining the tables directly that you need to gather the information you require. This way you are combining the real source of the data, and hopefully only making the exact joins needed.

This application was so complex, it actually took me about five weeks to even figure out what this expensive query was doing. Suffice it to say, I finally figured out what it needed, rewrote the query to not use any views, and the query went sub-second.

The team using that application had been used to clicking the SAVE button and going for a coffee break. This time, they clicked SAVE, and it was done. And they didn't even realize it. Once they did, they were ecstatic. They even gave me a little certificate award.

Yes, these are a couple war stories shared from my own experiences. But they are meant to convey a couple valuable points.

Data changes over time. The volume of rows in various tables can change over time, hence causing performance issues that weren't there before. Some operations aren't even critical path "mission critical" and can still eat up valuable resources.

The landscape of query writing is quite dynamic, and so being able to stop building new features and instead dig in and analyze and perform updates to fix dragging queries is always a valuable skill.

But it's not hard. Databases and SQL are quite approachable by any database user, which makes one ask, what is a database user?

WHAT IS A DATABASE USER?_

A prior colleague of mine who actually led the database development team on a contract once told me, "SQL isn't rocket science."

And he said that not to be snarky, but to call SQL for what it was. It's pretty simple.

That is why not only do application developers get it. But business analysts get it. Program managers get it. Many people if they indulge a little bit will get it.

Some of the rules we hear like "create an index" or "don't join views together" sometimes sound like they are being handed down from on high.

This book is meant to demystify all that and realize that with a few fundamentals about how relational databases operate, you can effect great change.

With these basic concepts, you can produce much. And let me tell you another truth: if you can make queries sizzle, you'll become a valued asset to your team. I can't promise you'll have a position forever at a given shop, but being able to extract information from a database is always useful.

There are many things we didn't cover. One of the biggest

is transactions. That's because transactions are a layer up, sitting on top of relational database concepts and basic SQL. Transactions also come with their own pros and cons. And that is a topic perhaps best covered in a future book.

If you enjoyed this book, I invite you to check out my YouTube channel https://youtube.com/@ProCoderIO. It's dedicated to helping pro coders enhance their skills in more ways than just writing better code.

Thanks,

—Greg

ABOUT THE AUTHOR_

Greg L. Turnquist worked on the Spring team for over thirteen years before he joined Cockroach Labs as a senior staff technical content engineer. He was the lead for Spring Data JPA, Spring Web Services, and a committer to Spring HATEOAS, Spring Data, Spring Boot, and R2DBC. He wrote Packt's best-selling title, *Learning Spring Boot 2.0 2nd Edition*, and its *3rd Edition* follow-up as well as *Hacking with Spring Boot 2.3: Reactive Edition* and other titles. He co-founded the Nashville Java User Group in 2010 and hasn't met a query, yet, that he can't speed up.

Signup at **procoder.io/whatisadatabase** and catch all of Greg's future works. You'll get a FREE technical handout as a bonus!

Be sure to subscribe to Pro Coder, the YouTube channel that helps you accelerate your coding career with actionable advice at **youtube.com/@ProCoderIO**.

ALSO BY GREG L. TURNQUIST_

Enjoy his other published works (**https://trnq.st/books**):

12 Rules For Pro Coders

Learning Spring Boot 3.0 3rd Edition

Hacking with Spring Boot 2.4: Classic Edition

Hacking with Spring Boot 2.3: Reactive Edition

Learning Spring Boot 2.0 2nd Edition

Learning Spring Boot

Python Testing Cookbook

Spring Python 1.1

Made in the USA
Monee, IL
05 November 2026

67378016R00052